W9-BZH-946

What if you were a Master Creator?

What if you were so good at creating, you could create anything you wanted from seemingly nothing at all?

What if you were so good at creation, creation started becoming dull? Although you had the admiration of world after world (some of which you helped create), you began to miss the challenge you felt earlier in your creative career.

So, Master Creator that you are, you created a button marked "Greater Challenge."

You considered all that might be contained in the concept of "Greater Challenge," decided Greater Challenge would probably provide some of the excitement and satisfaction you missed from your apprentice days, took a deep breath, pushed the button . . .

. . . and found yourself where you are right now—feeling what you're feeling now, thinking what you're thinking now, with everything in your life precisely the way it is now—reading this book.

Books by John-Roger and Peter McWilliams

You Can't Afford the Luxury of a Negative Thought:
A Book for People with Any Life-Threatening Illness—Including Life

Focus on the Positive:
The You Can't Afford the Luxury of a Negative Thought Workbook

LIFE 101:
Everything We Wish We Had Learned About Life In School—But Didn't

DO IT! Let's Get Off Our Buts

WEALTH 101: Wealth Is Much More Than Money

The Portable LIFE 101

The Portable DO IT!

All of the above titles are also available in unabridged audio format.

The Portable
DO IT!

172 essential excerpts plus 190 quotations
from the #1 *New York Times* bestseller
DO IT! Let's Get Off Our Buts

by John-Roger and Peter McWilliams

Prelude Press
8159 Santa Monica Boulevard
Los Angeles, California 90046
1-800-LIFE-101

ISBN 0-931580-81-1

Book design by Victoria Marine

Printed in the United States of America by Vaughan Printing

Introduction

(a very short one, in keeping with the brevity of this book)

The Portable DO IT! contains 172 essential excerpts from the text of the much longer book *DO IT! Let's Get Off Our Buts*. As Blaise Pascal once penned to a friend, "If I had more time, I would write a shorter letter." When we wrote the original *DO IT!*, we didn't have the time, so it was a longer book. We've now taken the time and created this more portable version.

If you read the full-sized *DO IT!* (we can't call it *"The Stationary DO IT!"* because *doing it* is never stationary), *The Portable DO IT!* will be a review, a traveling companion while fulfilling your dreams. If you haven't read the full-sized *DO IT!*, *The Portable DO IT!* will be a preview (a painless one, we trust). Also taken from the original *DO IT!* are 190 quotations from famous doers, past and present.

> *I might repeat to myself, slowly and soothingly,*
> *a list of quotations beautiful from minds profound—*
> *if I can remember any of the damn things.*
>
> DOROTHY PARKER

If you want to explore an idea more fully, at the bottom of each page, in the center, is a small number. This is the page number in the full-sized *DO IT!* from which the excerpt was taken. Turning to that page in the original *DO IT! Let's Get Off Our Buts* will give you a broader perspective on the excerpted thought.

Thanks for reading, and enjoy *doing it!*

John-Roger and Peter McWilliams

Page number from
the original *DO IT!*
will appear here

○

*I was going to buy a copy of
The Power of Positive Thinking,
and then I thought:
What the hell good would that do?*

RONNIE SHAKES

The Portable
DO IT!

*To achieve your goal,
your life may sound
like a perfume counter—
full of Passion and Obsession,
leading to Joy.*

1

We all have a dream, a heart's desire. Most have more than one. Some of us have an entire entourage. This is a book about discovering (or rediscovering) those dreams, how to choose which dreams to pursue, and practical suggestions for achieving them.

Properly, we should read for power.
Man reading should be man intensely alive.
The book should be a ball of light in one's hand.

EZRA POUND

3

2

By pursuing any *one* of our dreams, we can find fulfillment.
We don't need to pursue them all.

*As Miss America,
my goal is to bring peace
to the entire world
and then
to get my own apartment.*

JAY LENO

3

3

We don't have to *achieve* a dream in order to find fulfillment—we need only actively *pursue* the dream to attain satisfaction.

> *Regret for the things we did*
> *can be tempered by time;*
> *it is regret for the things we did not do*
> *that is inconsolable.*

SYDNEY J. HARRIS

3

4

By living our dream, we can contribute not only to ourselves, but to everyone and everything around us. And yet, most people are not pursuing their dreams.

> *There are some people*
> *that if they don't know,*
> *you can't tell 'em.*
>
> LOUIS ARMSTRONG

3

5

When we're not pursuing our dreams, we spend our time and abilities pursuing the things we *think* will make us happy, the things we *believe* will bring us fulfillment: the new house, the new car, the new cashmere jump suit.

You can't get enough of
what you don't really want.

3

6

Many people are so far away from living their dream that *they have forgotten what their dream truly is.*

Many of life's failures are
people who did not realize
how close they were to success
when they gave up.

THOMAS EDISON

3

7

It is sad. It is unnecessary. It is wasteful. And yet, it's so common an ailment that it's become a cliché. We have abandoned our heart's desire—and somewhere, deep down, we know it. Even if we don't remember quite what it is—we miss it.

> *"Let's Go."*
> *"Yes, let's go."*
> *Stage Direction: They do not move.*

LAST LINES OF
WAITING FOR GODOT
SAMUEL BECKETT

3

8

You may find the first part of this book depressing. We're going to explain why most people aren't living their dreams—and we're not going to pull any punches. It's not a pretty picture.

> *Facts do not cease to exist*
> *because they are ignored.*
>
> WILLIAM S. BURROUGHS

> *You have everything but one thing: madness.*
> *A man needs a little madness or else—*
> *he never dares cut the rope and be free.*
>
> ZORBA THE GREEK

13

*There are many who are living
far below their possibilities
because they are continually handing over
their individualities to others.
Do you want to be a power in the world?
Then be yourself.
Be true to the highest within your soul
and then allow yourself to be governed
by no customs or conventionalities
or arbitrary man-made rules
that are not founded on principle.*

RALPH WALDO TRINE

9

Why aren't we living our dreams? Because there is something we are trained to honor more than our dreams: **the comfort zone.**

*We act as though comfort and luxury
were the chief requirements of life,
when all that we need to make us happy
is something to be enthusiastic about.*

CHARLES KINGSLEY

5

10

The comfort zone is all the things we have done often enough to feel comfortable doing again. Whenever we do something new, it falls outside the barrier of the comfort zone. In even *contemplating* a new action, we feel fear, guilt, unworthiness, hurt feelings, and/or anger—all those emotions we generally think of as "uncomfortable."

*The only thing I can't stand
is discomfort.*

GLORIA STEINEM

5

11

When we feel uncomfortable enough long enough, we tend to feel discouraged (a form of exhaustion), and we return to thoughts, feelings and actions that are more familiar, more practiced, more predictable—more, well, comfortable.

It is hard to fight an enemy
who has outposts in your head.

SALLY KEMPTON

5

12

The irony is that the feelings we have been taught to label "uncomfortable" are, in fact, among the very tools necessary to fulfill our dreams. As it turns out, the bricks used to build the walls of the comfort zone are made of gold.

*Each handicap
is like a hurdle in a steeplechase,
and when you ride up to it,
if you throw your heart over,
the horse will go along, too.*

LAWRENCE BIXBY

5

13

We no longer believe in Santa Claus, but we still believe that "being uncomfortable" is reason enough not to do something new. The Easter Bunny hopped out of our lives years ago, yet we still let "what other people might think" affect our behavior. The tooth fairy was yanked from our consciousness long before adolescence, but we still feel we can justify any personal failure by finding someone or something outside ourselves to blame.

We're all in this alone.

LILY TOMLIN

5

14

Most people are drifting along in a childish sleep. To live our dreams, we must wake up.

Men stumble over the truth from time to time, but most pick themselves up and hurry off as if nothing happened.

SIR WINSTON CHURCHILL

Losing my virginity was a career move.

MADONNA

7

15

F. Scott Fitzgerald met Joan Crawford at a Hollywood party. He told her that he had been hired to write the screenplay for her next film. She looked him straight in the eye and said, "Write hard, Mr. Fitzgerald, write hard."

Imagine that we co-authors are looking you straight in the eye and saying, "Dream big, dear reader, dream big."

If you're not playing
a big enough game,
you'll screw up
the game you're playing
just to give yourself
something to do.

9

16

The truth is, pursuing a Big Dream of your own choosing
is the same amount of work as gathering more and more
of the things you don't really want. You're going to spend
the rest of your life doing *something*. It might as well be
something *you* want to do.

> *Ours is a world where people*
> *don't know what they want*
> *and are willing to go*
> *through hell to get it.*
>
> DON MARQUIS

9

17

The willingness to do creates the ability to do.

Where does the willingness come from?

From you.

As Joni Mitchell pointed out, "It all comes down to you."

We certainly agree, and would only add, "It all comes down to *do.*"

*Every creator painfully experiences the chasm
between his inner vision and its ultimate expression.*

ISAAC BASHEVIS SINGER

11

This is the true joy in life,
the being used for a purpose
recognized by yourself as a mighty one;
the being thoroughly worn out
before you are thrown on the scrap heap;
the being a force of nature
instead of a feverish selfish little clod
of ailments and grievances complaining
that the world will not devote itself
to making you happy.

GEORGE BERNARD SHAW

18

The reason we aren't living our dreams is *inside ourselves*. For the most part, however, we *pretend* it's people, things and situations *outside ourselves* that are to blame. (Not enough money, education, contacts, intelligence, looks, etc.)

Always listen to experts.
They'll tell you what
can't be done and why.
Then do it.

ROBERT HEINLEIN

13

19

When we know that the *cause* of something is in ourselves, and that we (ourselves) are one of the few things in this universe that we have the right and the ability to change, we begin to get a sense of the choices we really do have, an inkling of the power we have, a feeling of being in charge— of our lives, of our future, of our dreams.

> *They always say that*
> *time changes things,*
> *but you actually have to*
> *change them yourself.*
>
> ANDY WARHOL

13

20

But—that three-letter, four-letter word. When used in a sentence, "but" usually means: "Ignore all that good-sounding stuff that went before—here comes the truth." We might even consider BUT an acronym for *Behold the Underlying Truth*. (And BUTS can be shortened to BS.)

> *Do or do not.*
> *There is no try.*
>
> YODA

17

21

The naked "but" is what we use when ignoring our own good advice. When ignoring the unbearably good advice from another source, we use the hyphenated version: "yes-but." When we argue for our limitations, we get to keep them. *Yes-but* means, "Here come the arguments for my limitations." Or, if you favor acronyms . . .

YES-BUT = *Your Evaluation is Superb— Behold the Underlying Truth.*

Advice is what we ask for when we already know the answer but wish we didn't.

ERICA JONG

19

22

In any given area of life, we have one of two things: reasons or results—excuses or experiences, stories or successes, justifications or justice. We either have what we want, or we have ironclad, airtight, impenetrable reasons why it was not even *marginally possible* to get it.

Success is simply
a matter of luck.
Ask any failure.

EARL WILSON

21

23

We've been programmed to use one of the most powerful tools *at* our disposal—the mind—*for* our disposal. Rather than dispose of the barriers to our dreams, the mind disposes of the dreams.

> *In the choice between*
> *changing one's mind*
> *and proving there's*
> *no need to do so,*
> *most people get busy*
> *on the proof.*

JOHN KENNETH GALBRAITH

21

24

In the amount of time it takes for the mind to invent a good excuse, it could have created an alternate way of achieving the desired result—rendering excuse-making unnecessary.

Quit now, you'll never make it.
If you disregard this advice,
you'll be halfway there.

DAVID ZUCKER

21

25

Let's take a closer look at the comfort zone—fear, guilt, unworthiness, hurt feelings, anger and discouragement. (Just what you wanted, huh?)

Minds, like bodies,
will often fall into a
pimpled, ill-conditioned state
from mere excess of comfort.

CHARLES DICKENS

31

26

Because it's so common, **fear** has many other names: apprehension, misgiving, trepidation, dread, horror, phobia, terror, alarm, consternation, foreboding, qualm, suspicion, fret, uneasiness, distress, panic, worry, and so on.

I'm a paranoiac, baby,
so I hope you don't make the mistake
of laboring under the false impression
that you are talking to a sane person.

TENNESSEE WILLIAMS

33

27

Physically, we feel fear in the area we generally call the stomach. Although it's lower than the physical stomach (more in the area of the lower abdomen), for the sake of locating fear—and going along with the popular use of the word—we'll define "the stomach" as a large, circular area with the navel at its center. (Guilt hangs out there too.)

> *Fear is the main source of superstition,*
> *and one of the main sources of cruelty.*
> *To conquer fear*
> *is the beginning of wisdom.*
>
> BERTRAND RUSSELL

33

28

Someone once described FEAR in an acronym: *F*alse *Expectations Appearing Real*. For the most part, what we fear is not real—it is merely our mind *imagining* something awful that has not yet happened.

Fear is pain arising from the anticipation of evil.
ARISTOTLE

To him who is in fear, everything rustles.
SOPHOCLES

33

29

Seldom do we do the thing we fear, so we seldom discover if our projection of disaster is accurate. In fact, when we *don't* do the thing we are afraid of, we breathe a sigh of relief *as though it actually would have taken place.* "That was a *close* one!" we say, even though we never actually got *close* to anything but a string of our own negative thoughts. Fear breeds lack of experience, lack of experience breeds ignorance (ignore-ance), ignorance breeds more fear. It is a vicious circle.

> *You can't expect to hit the jackpot*
> *if you don't put a few nickels in the machine.*
> FLIP WILSON

32

30

Put another way, fear is interest paid on a debt you may not owe.

*Fear is that little darkroom
where negatives are developed.*

MICHAEL PRITCHARD

35

31

Guilt is the anger we feel toward ourselves when we do something "wrong." The trouble is, most of us haven't really explored what *we* think is truly "right" and "wrong" in years—maybe ever.

> *The only reason I feel guilty*
> *about masturbation*
> *is that I do it so badly.*
>
> DAVID STEINBERG

39

32

The process of limitation and immobility is *fear before* we do something new, and *guilt after.* (Maybe that's why they're both felt in the area of the stomach.) Guilt is the remorse—the shame, the regret—we feel at having done something "different." We feel so bad we promise ourselves, "I'll never do that again!" even if it's the very thing we need to do, over and over.

> *Last night at twelve I felt immense,*
> *But now I feel like thirty cents.*

GEORGE ADE
1902

39

33

Guilt can rewrite the *memory* of an experience. We may do something new, enjoy the doing of it (or the result of doing it), and guilt will actually convince us that we didn't like it (or got nothing from it). We can say to someone, "I'm not going to do that again; I didn't really like it," and believe it—although, in fact, the experience itself (not the fear before the experience or the guilt after, but the *actual experience itself*) was enjoyable (or profitable).

If you're going to do something wrong, at least enjoy it.

LEO ROSTEN

39

34

Unworthiness is the deep-seated belief we have about ourselves that tells us we're undeserving, not good enough, inadequate, and fundamentally deficient.

You have no idea
what a poor opinion
I have of myself—
and how little I deserve it.

W. S. GILBERT

43

35

Unworthiness is the primal doubt we feel in the pit of our stomach when we consider living a dream.

"Don't try it," unworthiness warns.

"Don't even *think* about it."

And so, we don't even think about it. Our mind goes off on one distraction after another—anything rather than having to face even the *possibility* of our own elemental inadequacy.

Our doubts are traitors, and make us lose the good
we oft might win by fearing to attempt.

SHAKESPEARE

43

36

Physically, unworthiness resides in the area of the solar plexus—an area just below the breast bone where the rib cage forms an inverted "V". In some Eastern traditions, they call this the center of *Chi*, a fundamental point for focusing energy and moving ahead in life. Unworthiness inhibits that energy.

The wonderful thing about saints is that they were human.
They lost their tempers, scolded God,
were egotistical or testy or impatient in their turns,
made mistakes and regretted them.
Still they went on doggedly blundering toward heaven.

PHYLLIS McGINLEY

43

37

One of the most popular of unworthiness's comments, however, is, upon hearing of our own good fortune, "I don't believe it! That's too good to be true!" It's often spoken with such enthusiasm—and such self-limitation—that the good that's "unbelievable" soon disappears.

> *The world is moving so fast these days*
> *that the man who says*
> *it can't be done*
> *is generally interrupted*
> *by someone doing it.*

HARRY EMERSON FOSDICK

45

38

When we don't get what we want from others, when they fail to keep their promises, when they let us down, we often have **hurt feelings.**

Even deeper (and more frequent) are the times we have let *ourselves* down. That hurts too.

> *There is no security on this earth,*
> *there is only opportunity.*
>
> GENERAL DOUGLAS MACARTHUR

47

39

A common "cover-up" for hurt is **anger.** We blame whatever or whoever let us down, and we get *steamed.* ("How *dare* you!") Some people have anger as the *automatic response* to disappointment. In almost all cases, however, hurt is just underneath.

> *I buy women shoes,*
> *and they use them*
> *to walk away from me.*
>
> MICKEY ROONEY

47

40

Another common defense against hurt is depression. Some people feel so *down* all the time that one more hurt is just another drop in the ocean of their melancholy. (Remember, much of this is not logical by adult standards.)

I know a man who gave up smoking,
drinking, sex, and rich food.
He was healthy right up to the time he killed himself.

JOHNNY CARSON

Your request for no MSG was ignored.

FORTUNE COOKIE

47

41

After enough hurt and anger (and depression), people tend to decide, "I'm not going to do anything that causes me any more pain." That would, of course, include any behavior of a dream-fulfillment nature.

*You have to leave the city of your comfort
and go into the wilderness of your intuition.
What you'll discover will be wonderful.
What you'll discover will be yourself.*

ALAN ALDA

47

42

Over time, the result of all this fear, guilt, unworthiness, hurt feelings and anger is **discouragement.** Discouragement promotes inaction, and inaction guarantees failure—a life of not living our dreams.

*Discouragement is simply
the despair of
wounded self-love.*

FRANÇOIS DE FÈNELON

49

43

It's hard to imagine anything more pernicious—and effective—than discouragement. Although we, as adults, have the power we didn't have as children to pursue our dreams, discouragement keeps us from using it.

> *Basically, my wife was immature.*
> *I'd be at home in the bath*
> *and she'd come in*
> *and sink my boats.*

> WOODY ALLEN

49

44

Our parents (or whoever raised us) *loved* us—in the most fundamental sense of that word. Maybe they didn't hug us all we wanted, but they *fed* us, *clothed* us and physically nurtured us such that we are at least alive today.

> *I don't know any parents*
> *who look into the eyes*
> *of a newborn baby and say,*
> *"How can we screw this kid up?"*

RUSSELL BISHOP

57

45

The major reasons parents don't raise their children free from trauma are

1. Parents don't know any better.

2. Children require different rules than adults.

3. Parents have other things to do besides raising children (like dealing with money, each other, and life).

4. Who on earth knows what a child needs when?

If you want a place in the sun,
you must leave the shade of the family tree.

OSAGE SAYING

57

46

The bad news about the comfort zone: The comfort zone is never static. It is either expanding or contracting. If you're not consciously expanding the comfort zone, it contracts.

In the heating and air conditioning trade,
the point on the thermostat in which
neither heating nor cooling must operate
—around 72 degrees—
is called "The Comfort Zone."
It's also known as "The Dead Zone."

RUSSELL BISHOP

69

47

The worst news about the comfort zone: The comfort zone is not just a collection of "uncomfortable" emotions—it has its own personality, character and individuality. It is a complex psychological-physiological entity unto itself.

> *Don't try to take on a new personality;*
> *it doesn't work.*
>
> RICHARD NIXON

71

48

Many don't see the comfort zone as a limitation at all. They call it "intuition," "morality," or "conscience." Some connect it with *religion*—they think the limiting rantings of the comfort zone are the voice of God.

(We won't even discuss what happens when these people put their self-limitations on others—by force, if necessary. Well, take a look at history; take a look *around!)*

A great many people think they are thinking when they are merely rearranging their prejudices.

WILLIAM JAMES

71

49

The comfort zone knows us intimately and hits us at our weakest point. It wouldn't dream of using an excuse we could see through. It uses the reasons we find reasonable, the rationales we find rational (the "rational lies"), the realizations we find most real ("real lies"). It takes our greatest aspirations and turns them into excuses for not bothering to aspire.

My idea of an agreeable person
is a person who agrees with me.

BENJAMIN DISRAELI

71

Good behavior is the last refuge of mediocrity.

HENRY S. HASKINS

If you have a job without aggravations,
you don't have a job.

MALCOM FORBES

50

The even worse news about the comfort zone: To the degree we're not living our dreams, our comfort zone has more control of us than we have over ourselves.

Human beings yield in many situations,
even important and spiritual and central ones,
as long as it prolongs one's well-being.
ALEXANDER SOLZHENITSYN

73

*One can never consent to creep
when one feels
an impulse to soar.*

HELEN KELLER

51

The very worst news about the comfort zone: In order to truly master the comfort zone, we have to learn to love it.

> *Love your enemies*
> *just in case*
> *your friends turn out to be*
> *a bunch of bastards.*

R. A. DICKSON

75

52

The good news about the comfort zone: All the energy that makes up the comfort zone is *yours*.

Men are born to succeed, not to fail.

HENRY DAVID THOREAU

If you want a quality,
act as if you already had it.
Try the "as if" technique.

WILLIAM JAMES

79

53

We are built for success. We're programmed for failure, perhaps, but we're built for success.

Use your weaknesses;
aspire to the strength.
SIR LAURENCE OLIVIER

77

54

Fear, guilt, unworthiness, hurt feelings and anger are, of course, *emotions*. Emotion is *energy* in *motion*. We take *our energy* and put it in *motion*. Sometimes it's joy, sometimes it's sorrow; sometimes it's guilt, sometimes it's pride; sometimes it's pain, sometimes it's pleasure—whatever the emotion, the energy that's in motion *is what we put in motion*.

> *My grandmother started walking*
> *five miles a day when she was sixty.*
> *She's ninety-five now,*
> *and we don't know where the hell she is.*

ELLEN DeGENERES

79

55

People often want to "get rid of" a "negative" emotion—
fear, say, or unworthiness—before attempting something
new. That's the same thing as saying, "I want to get rid of
some of my energy."

It's all right to have
butterflies in your stomach.
Just get them to fly in formation.

DR. ROB GILBERT

79

56

Fear, guilt, unworthiness, hurt feelings and anger are, in fact, *tools*. Tools are neutral—they can be used either *for* us, or *against* us. A knife can be used to heal or to hurt. A hammer can be used to build or to destroy. It is not the tool itself, but *the way the tool is used* that determines its benefit or detriment.

> *They shall beat their swords into plowshares,*
> *and their spears into pruning hooks:*
> *nation shall not lift up sword against nation,*
> *neither shall they learn war any more.*

ISAIAH 2:4

79

57

Imagine if all the energy of fear, guilt, unworthiness, hurt feelings and anger were available to help us achieve anything we wanted.

Well, it is.

> *I know God will not give me*
> *anything I can't handle.*
> *I just wish that*
> *He didn't trust me so much.*
>
> MOTHER TERESA

81

58

It's as though someone hung a large rock around our neck. "Oh, how heavy," we'd complain. Later we were told the rock was really a diamond in the rough. "Oh! How heavy!" we'd exclaim. Fear, guilt, unworthiness, hurt feelings and anger are diamonds in the rough. They're valuable now, and with a little cutting and polishing, they become priceless.

We must select the illusion
which appeals to our temperament
and embrace it with passion,
if we want to be happy.

CYRIL CONNOLLY

81

When such as I cast out remorse
So great a sweetness flows into the breast
We must laugh and we must sing,
We are blest by everything,
Everything we look upon is blest.

WILLIAM BUTLER YEATS

59

Fear is the energy to do your best in a new situation.

Try a thing you haven't done three times.
Once, to get over the fear of doing it.
Twice, to learn how to do it.
And a third time to figure out
whether you like it or not.

VIRGIL THOMSON

83

60

Contrary to popular belief, our parents didn't teach us to feel fear. Our parents *did* teach us to use fear as a reason *not* to do something. Children cannot logically determine if their physical well-being is or is not endangered when attempting each new activity, but adults can.

Society attacks early,
when the individual is helpless.

B. F. SKINNER

83

61

Once you know something is not physically dangerous, go ahead and *do* the thing. It may feel uncomfortable (count on it), but keep moving one step after another in the direction of doing it.

As you move—as you *use it*—the energy will transform itself from barrier to blessing. You'll have *energy*, not limitation.

There are risks and costs to a program of action,
but they are far less than the long-range risks
and costs of comfortable inaction.

JOHN F. KENNEDY

85

     Let's Get Off Our Buts

62

This process of feeling the fear and doing it anyway reprograms our attitude from, "Fear means, 'Don't' " to "Fear means, 'All systems go!' "

You gain strength, courage and confidence
by every experience in which
you really stop to look fear in the face.
You are able to say to yourself,
"I lived through this horror.
I can take the next thing that comes along."
You must do the thing you think you cannot do.

ELEANOR ROOSEVELT

85

63

Guilt is the energy for personal change.

The wages of sin are death,
but by the time taxes are taken out,
it's just sort of a tired feeling.

PAULA POUNDSTONE

87

64

When we feel guilty, and want to use the anger directed at ourselves for change (for a change), we have two options: we can either change our *actions,* or change our *beliefs* about those actions.

> *Everything I did in my life*
> *that was worthwhile*
> *I caught hell for.*
>
> EARL WARREN

87

65

There's a lot of energy available in the anger of guilt. It's a matter of remembering to redirect it from *blame* to *change—over and over.*

> *Destiny is not a matter of chance;*
> *it is a matter of choice.*
> *It is not a thing to be waited for;*
> *it is a thing to be achieved.*

WILLIAM JENNINGS BRYAN

66

When used to produce guilt, the statement, "I could have done better!" is false. If we *knew* better we'd *do* better.

A more accurate statement when we *intellectually* "knew better" (and did it anyway) is to say, "This will remind me to do better next time—I'm still learning." Because, of course, we are.

*Show me a guy who's afraid to look bad
and I'll show you a guy you can beat every time.*

RENE AUBERJONOIS

93

67

Unworthiness keeps us on track.

*There are three reasons why
lawyers are replacing rats
as laboratory research animals.
One is that they're plentiful,
another is that lab assistants
don't get attached to them,
and the third is that
there are some things
rats just won't do.*

95

68

Worthiness and unworthiness keep us on our path. It is our path. We selected it—it leads to our dream. Unworthiness is a friend that says, "Your path is this way, not that way." Be content knowing that your dream is yours, and accept that everything that's not your dream is not yours.

Seen in this way, the feeling of unworthiness is better described as *humility*. We know what we want, we know the direction we're going, we know that we are entitled to our dream, and we let the rest of the goals go by.

Being a newspaper columnist is like being married to
a nymphomaniac. It's great for the first two weeks.

LEWIS GRIZZARD

97

69

Hurt feelings are a reminder of how much we care and anger is the energy for change.

Don't go around saying
the world owes you a living;
the world owes you nothing;
it was here first.

MARK TWAIN

99

70

Beneath hurt is caring. The depth of the hurt indicates the depth of the caring. The anger that hides the hurting shows the degree of caring, too.

Vex not thy spirit at the course of things;
they heed not thy vexation.
How ludicrous and outlandish is astonishment
at anything that may happen in life.

MARCUS AURELIUS

99

Oh God,
in the name of Thine
only beloved Son,
Jesus Christ, Our Lord,
let him phone me <u>now</u>.

DOROTHY PARKER

71

Another word for caring, of course, is **love.** Love is powerful. Keep it directed toward your goal. Most people use hurt as a reason to stop. Then you truly *are* hurt; you hurt yourself—you keep yourself from attaining your heart's desire. You do that by stopping.

> *When love and skill work together,*
> *expect a masterpiece.*
>
> JOHN RUSKIN

99

72

Feel the *passion* of the caring. Put that behind your goal. If you feel *anger*, remember this is the energy for change. *Use* it; *do* something with it. Even if you can't do anything physically, use the energy to *imagine* success.

> *The ancestor of every action is a thought.*
> RALPH WALDO EMERSON

99

73

Our *feelings* don't say stop—our *programming* says stop. It's time to rewrite that programming to say, "Here's the information and the energy necessary to course-correct and continue moving toward your dreams."

Very few people possess true artistic ability.
It is therefore both unseemly and unproductive
to irritate the situation by making an effort.
If you have a burning, restless urge to write or paint,
simply eat something sweet and the feeling will pass.

FRAN LEBOWITZ

101

74

This is the power of the **imagination:** we can return to the past, rehearse the future, and zoom off on flights of fancy—all within seconds. The imagination is for rehearsing our dreams and reliving our joys.

*I can believe anything,
provided it is incredible.*

OSCAR WILDE

117

75

When the comfort zone has control of the imagination, it is vigorously and creatively used *against* us. We relive the horrors of the past—the fears that were justified, the guilts that were especially foul, the unworthinesses at their worst, the hurt feelings at their most painful, the anger at its most destructive.

*The longer I live the more I see
that I am never wrong about anything,
and that all the pains I have so humbly taken
to verify my notions have only wasted my time.*

GEORGE BERNARD SHAW

117

76

Evict it! Out! Your imagination is yours. You can remember the past you choose, rehearse the future you want, and identify with the real and fictional heroes and events of your selection.

> *I am looking for a lot of men*
> *who have an infinite capacity*
> *to not know what can't be done.*
>
> HENRY FORD

119

The way you activate the seeds of your creation
is by making choices
about the results you want to create.
When you make a choice,
you mobilize vast human energies and resources
which otherwise go untapped.
All too often people fail to focus
their choices upon results
and therefore their choices are ineffective.
If you limit your choices only to
what seems possible or reasonable,
you disconnect yourself
from what you truly want,
and all that is left
is a compromise.

ROBERT FRITZ

77

Often, what we *really* want is hidden beneath what we've settled for. When the comfort zone doesn't allow the expanded behavior necessary to fulfill our dream, we tend to forget the dream. It's too painful otherwise. When we know we *can* have what we want—that the comfort zone is under *our* control—we can remember what it is we truly want.

Poor is the man whose pleasures
depend on the permission of another.

MADONNA

133

78

A **goal** is what we want. **Methods** are the ways of getting it. A goal is our heart's desire. Methods are the *actions, information, things* and *behaviors* we use to get it.

*Strong lives are motivated
by dynamic purposes.*

KENNETH HILDEBRAND

147

79

When you ask some people why they're not living their dream, they usually respond with a listing of unavailable methods: not enough money, looks, information, contacts, breaks, etc. All these are just methods. They may sound like rational reasons, but they are, in reality, just rational lies.

Perfections of means and confusion of goals seem
—in my opinion—
to characterize our age.

ALBERT EINSTEIN

147

80

Most people let their methods decide their goals. This is a fundamental mistake in manifestation. Those who look at what they already *have* before selecting what they *want* are concerned with *making do,* not *doing.*

> *The great thing in this world*
> *is not so much where we are,*
> *but in what direction we are moving.*

OLIVER WENDELL HOLMES

147

81

The reason many people feel bored and unfulfilled is that they spend their lives shuffling and reshuffling the methods they already have. This can be like rearranging deck chairs on the Titanic—no matter how well it's done, the result is the same. As someone said, "If you do what you've always done, you'll get what you've always gotten."

*One doesn't discover new lands without consenting to
lose sight of the shore for a very long time.*

ANDRÉ GIDE

147

82

When choosing a dream, look to your heart, not to your "reality." That's why it's called a dream. Make that dream your goal. Commit to it. Act upon that commitment. The methods to fulfill that dream will appear.

Follow your bliss.
JOSEPH CAMPBELL

83

Selfing means doing for one's Self, in the larger sense of Self, as in True Self, or "To thine own self be true." It means fulfilling the dreams, goals and aspirations inherent within us. It means living our life "on purpose."

> *This above all:*
> *to thine own self be true,*
> *And it must follow,*
> *as the night the day,*
> *Thou canst not then be false*
> *to any man.*

SHAKESPEARE

157

84

Selfish, on the other hand, is the petty, endlessly greedy gathering of stuff (houses, cars, boats, clothes), stuff (husbands, wives, children, lovers), and more stuff (power, fame, money, sex). It's the relentless pursuit of glamour at all costs. It's worshiping the god of other people's opinion.

> *The only man who is really free*
> *is the one who can turn down*
> *an invitation to dinner*
> *without giving an excuse.*
>
> JULES RENARD

157

85

Selfing is knowing what you want—what *you* want, not what you *should* want because others *say* you should want it, but what *you* want—and moving toward it.

Others may call you selfish, but you know that you are selfing—"being yourself."

We forfeit three-fourths of ourselves
to be like other people.

ARTHUR SCHOPENHAUER
(1788–1860)

157

86

You can have *anything* you want, but you can't have *everything* you want.

The important thing in acting
is to be able to laugh and cry.
If I have to cry,
I think of my sex life.
If I have to laugh,
I think of my sex life.

GLENDA JACKSON

161

87

You can have *anything* you want: No dream is too big to achieve. If *one other* person has achieved it, you can be the second. If *no other* person has achieved it, you can be the first. Dream big, dear reader, dream big.

If someone says "can't,"
that shows you what to do.

JOHN CAGE

161

88

But you can't have *everything* you want: We live in a finite world for a finite period of time, but with an infinite imagination. Our imagination can create more wants than a computer can generate random numbers. We're not going to have time for all the wants we want.

> *When the eagles are silent*
> *the parrots begin to jabber.*
> SIR WINSTON CHURCHILL

161

89

The biggest lie in choosing is, "I can't."

That is simply not true.

The next time you hear yourself saying, to another—and especially to yourself—"I can't," take a deep breath and say instead, "My resources are otherwise engaged."

Because that's the truth.

Always do sober what you said you'd do drunk.
That will teach you to keep your mouth shut.

ERNEST HEMINGWAY

165

90

When choosing a dream to follow, it's good to consider the four basic areas in which people live. They are

Marriage/Family
Career/Professional
Social/Political
Religious/Spiritual

Happiness?
A good cigar, a good meal,
and a good woman—or a bad woman.
It depends on how much happiness you can handle.

GEORGE BURNS

167

91

Naturally, in the course of a lifetime, people tend to spend some time in each category. Looking back, however, most people can say, "Yes, I gave the majority of my time and attention to _____" and mention one of the categories. Sometimes, it's the area they *wanted* to spend most of their time in. This is satisfaction. Other times, they spent their life in an area *other* than the one closest to their heart. This hurts.

> *Here is the test to find whether*
> *your mission on earth is finished.*
> *If you're alive, it isn't.*
>
> RICHARD BACH

167

92

In choosing *now* which area you feel most drawn to, you can either (A) spend more time in that area, or (B) realize that the draw you feel ("I really *want* to do this, but I think I *should* do that") is from programming other than your own. Now is a good time to reprogram yourself so that the goals you follow are your own.

I once complained to my father that I didn't seem to be able to do things the same way other people did. Dad's advice? "Margo, don't be a sheep. People hate sheep. They eat sheep."

MARGO KAUFMAN

167

93

We're not sure whether all work and no play made Jack a dull boy, or whether Jack was a dull boy to begin with, so, dullard that he was, he worked too much. Either way, **fun** and **recreation** are a necessary part of an undull life.

Lots of folks confuse bad management with destiny.

KIN HUBBARD

*Cats are intended to teach us
that not everything in nature
has a function.*

GARRISON KEILLOR

197

94

When we say *recreation,* we mean it in the lighter sense of recreation (tennis, boating, going to the movies), as well as in the deeper sense—*re-creation.* What do you do to "re-create" yourself? This might include meditation, retreats *(re-treats),* prayer, spiritual work, rest, pilgrimages, massage, silent time—whatever activities recharge your batteries in a deep and powerful way.

> *How beautiful it is to do nothing,*
> *and then rest afterward.*
>
> SPANISH PROVERB

197

95

It's important to realize, however, that the endless pursuit of fun and recreation *in and of themselves* is not very fulfilling. In fact, it's something of a curse. When one pursues pleasure *all the time,* the pursuit of pleasure becomes work—it's a job.

*I can think of nothing less pleasurable
than a life devoted to pleasure.*

JOHN D. ROCKEFELLER, JR.

197

96

We didn't include Fun/Recreation in the other areas of life because we assume this is an area people will want to enjoy no matter what other area of life they choose. To use the analogy of a battery, Fun/Recreation charges the batteries; Marriage/Family, Career/Professional, Social/Political, and Religious/Spiritual are the ways in which the batteries are used.

> *The only true happiness*
> *comes from squandering ourselves*
> *for a purpose.*
>
> WILLIAM COWPER

197

97

Relationships are essential to the pursuit of almost any goal. In successfully achieving a goal, however, it is important to understand the different *types* of relationships that are available. When you do, you can see which types of relationships can best help you pursue your dream.

> *A Code of Honor—Never approach a friend's*
> *girlfriend or wife with mischief as your goal.*
> *There are just too many women in the world*
> *to justify that sort of dishonorable behavior.*
> *Unless she's <u>really</u> attractive.*

BRUCE JAY FRIEDMAN

199

98

Before exploring the types of relationships humans tend to have, here are two essential points about relationships in general. First, *all relationships are with yourself*—and sometimes they involve other people. Second, *the most important relationship in your life*—the one you'll have, like it or not, until the day you die—*is with yourself.*

> *Among those whom I like or admire,*
> *I can find no common denominator,*
> *but among those whom I love, I can:*
> *all of them make me laugh.*
>
> W. H. AUDEN

199

99

Recreational Relationships: These are the people we enjoy being with simply because we enjoy being with them. *What* we do together is not as important as *that we are* together.

> *We don't love qualities.*
> *We love a person;*
> *sometimes by reason of their defects*
> *as well as their qualities.*
>
> JACQUES MARITAIN

199

100

Romantic Relationships: Here, sex (or sexual desire) combines with a feeling of "you are the only one for me," and "if you don't love me, I'm miserable and worthless." We don't have to like—or even *know*—the "love object." Some say ignorance is a *prerequisite* for romantic love.

*Of course it is possible to love a human being,
if you don't know them too well.*

CHARLES BUKOWSKI

101

Contractual Relationships: In a contractual relationship, something is exchanged for something else. The "something" could be anything—a product, a service, an experience. Usually the culturally agreed upon *symbol for energy*—money—is involved in the transaction.

> *Almost all of our relationships begin*
> *and most of them continue*
> *as forms of mutual exploitation,*
> *a mental or physical barter,*
> *to be terminated when*
> *one or both parties run out of goods.*

W. H. AUDEN

203

102

Common-Goal Relationships: Here people share a common goal, and that goal is the primary reason they relate. This is often the source of work-based relationships. The common goal may be a company goal, a personal goal fulfilled by the company, or, simply, as Sir Noel Coward put it, "your pay packet at the end of the week."

*The value of marriage is not
that adults produce children,
but that children produce adults.*

PETER DE VRIES

205

103

Power-Point Relationships: This is a specific form of common-goal relationships. Here one person (or team of people) becomes the "power point." A group feeds its energy (power) to the power-point person (or team), and through this power point, the entire group can fulfill its common goal.

If the point is sharp, and the arrow is swift,
it can pierce through the dust no matter how thick.

BOB DYLAN

205

104

There are few "pure" relationships—most cross lines, combining one type of relationship with another. Relationships also change over time, evolving—or deteriorating—from one type to another. Knowing the type of relationships that are available helps you choose the type of relationships that will allow you to best fulfill your dreams.

My parents have been visiting me for a few days.
I just dropped them off at the airport.
They leave tomorrow.

MARGARET SMITH

209

I've been promoted to middle management.
I never thought I'd sink so low.

TIM GOULD

Never keep up with the Joneses.
Drag them down to your level.
It's cheaper.

QUENTIN CRISP

I don't know much about
being a millionaire,
but I'll bet I'd be <u>darling</u> at it.

DOROTHY PARKER

105

Money, fame and power—for their own sake—all spell one thing: *glamour.*

Glamour is one of the biggest traps in life. It is a sweet, sticky snare, like the petals of a Venus-flytrap. "Come to me," it beckons. "All happiness lies here."

What's money? A man is a success
if he gets up in the morning
and goes to bed at night
and in between does what he wants to do.

BOB DYLAN

233

*I travel light;
as light, that is,
as a man can travel
who will still
carry his body around
because of its sentimental value.*

CHRISTOPHER FRY

106

Are we saying money, fame and power are intrinsically evil? No. They have their place. They are tools—*methods* for obtaining other goals. As goals themselves, however, they are nothing. Less than nothing. Distractions at best; addictions at worst.

A celebrity is a person who
works hard all his life
to become well known,
then wears dark glasses
to avoid being recognized.

FRED ALLEN

233

107

Elementary school

2 + 2 = 4

College

$E = mc^2$

Life

TIME = DREAMS

Men, for the sake of getting a living, forget to live.
MARGARET FULLER

243

108

What do you want?

*What would you attempt to do
if you knew you could not fail?*

DR. ROBERT SCHULLER

245

109

Put something countable, something quantifiable in your goal so that you'll *know* when you've obtained it. You are not stuck with this goal forever and ever. When you reach it, you can choose a bigger one. For now, however, it's important to know *what* your goal is, and be able to tell *when* you've reached it.

*You've got to be very careful
if you don't know where you are going,
because you might not get there.*

YOGI BERRA

257

110

In order to have something new, our comfort zone must be expanded to include that new thing. The bigger the new thing, the greater the comfort zone must expand. And *comfort zones are most often expanded through discomfort.*

> *Do not be too timid and squeamish*
> *about your actions.*
> *All life is an experiment.*
>
> RALPH WALDO EMERSON

277

111

Committing to a dream is not a one-time occurrence. It must be done daily, hourly, continually. We must *choose* to commit to our *choice,* over and over.

*In the afternoons, Gertrude Stein and I used to go
antique hunting in the local shops,
and I remember once asking her
if she thought I should become a writer.
In the typically cryptic way we were all enchanted with,
she said, "No."
I took that to mean yes
and sailed for Italy the next day.*

WOODY ALLEN

279

112

The test of commitment is *action.* If we say, "I commit to being a great dancer," and then don't practice, that's not a commitment; that's just talk.

Never take a solemn oath.
People think you mean it.

NORMAN DOUGLAS

281

113

When we commit and act, we are confronted by the comfort zone. The temptation is to stop. If we move ahead *anyway,* we expand the comfort zone, learn a necessary lesson, and the commitment becomes stronger. That causes us to come up against the comfort zone again, and the process continues. Yes, it's uncomfortable, but (A) you'll get what you want and (B) in addition to what you want, you'll have an expanded comfort zone.

> *If you never want to see a man again, say,*
> *"I love you, I want to marry you.*
> *I want to have children . . ."*
> *—they leave skid marks.*

RITA RUDNER

281

114

Here are some suggestions for making and keeping commitments:

1. Don't make commitments you don't plan to keep.

2. Learn to say no.

3. Make conditional agreements. ("If . . . then . . .")

4. Keep the commitments you make.

5. Write commitments down. (Keep a calendar.)

6. If conflicts arise, renegotiate at the earliest opportunity.

Eighty percent of success is showing up.

WOODY ALLEN

281

Until one is committed,
there is hesitancy,
the chance to draw back,
always ineffectiveness.
Concerning all acts of initiative
(and creation)
there is one elementary truth,
the ignorance of which
kills countless ideas and splendid plans:
that the moment one definitely commits oneself,
then Providence moves too.
All sorts of things occur to help one
that would never otherwise have occurred.

*A whole stream of events
issues from the decision,
raising in one's favor
all manner of unforeseen incidents
and meetings and material assistance,
which no man could have dreamed
would have come his way.*

*I have learned a deep respect
for one of Goethe's couplets:*

**Whatever you can do, or dream you can, begin it.
Boldness has genius, power and magic in it.**

W. H. MURRAY
THE SCOTTISH HIMALAYAN EXPEDITION

115

It's important to commit to the fulfillment of the goal, not just to a certain amount of time spent pursuing the goal. When we commit to *pursuing,* our goal is then *pursuing,* and we will pursue. We won't necessarily *get* what we're pursuing, because getting it is not our goal—pursuing it is.

I always wanted to be somebody,
but I should have been more specific.

LILY TOMLIN

285

116

The time to commit is now.

    And now.

        And now.

            And now.

                And now.

                    And now.

                        And now.

                            And now.

                                And now . . .

287

117

Keep your goals away from the trolls.

It is a mistake for a sculptor or a painter
to speak or write very often about his job.
It releases the tension needed for his work.

HENRY MOORE

Give not which is holy unto the dogs,
neither cast ye your pearls before swine,
lest they trample them under their feet,
and turn again and rend you.

JESUS OF NAZARETH
MATTHEW 7:6

289

118

People don't like to see others pursuing their dreams—it reminds them how far from living their dreams they are. In talking you out of your dreams, they are talking themselves back into their own comfort zone. They will give you every rational lie they ever gave themselves.

> *These are the soul cages.*
> *These are the soul cages.*
> *Swim to the light.*
>
> STING

291

119

When you've obtained your goal, *then* tell others about it. Even though faced with irrefutable evidence, the most common expression you'll hear will be, "I don't believe it!" If they can't believe reality, imagine how much difficulty they'd have believing in your Dream.

> *Losers visualize the penalties of failure.*
> *Winners visualize the rewards of success.*
>
> DR. ROB GILBERT

120

To **affirm** is to *make firm.* An affirmation is a statement of truth you make firm by repetition. Affirmations help you believe in your Dream. Belief is essential. Your Dream must become more real than your doubt. Affirmations are like lifting weights—a mechanical process that helps build strength (belief) in your Dream.

*I used to work at The International House of Pancakes.
It was a dream, and I made it happen.*

PAULA POUNDSTONE

301

*Your automatic creative mechanism
operates in terms of goals and end results.
Once you give it a definite goal to achieve,
you can depend on its automatic guidance system
to take you to that goal much better
than "You" ever could by conscious thought.
"You" supply the goal
by thinking in terms of end results.
Your automatic mechanism
then supplies the means whereby.*

MAXWELL MALTZ

121

When we realize that our heroes became heroes *flaws and all,* it gives us hope. "You mean we don't have to be perfect to fulfill our Dream, to make a contribution?" Hardly. It takes commitment, courage and passion to live a dream and make a contribution. Heroes had these qualities *along with* their flaws. And you have those qualities, too.

> *Have I ever told you you're my hero?*
> *You're everything I would like to be.*
> *I can climb higher than an eagle.*
> *You are the wind beneath my wings.*

LARRY HENLEY
JEFF SILBAR

309

122

Within our bodies is the energy of individual creation. We call this **achievement energy.** People experience achievement energy differently depending on what they call it. Just as a certain energy in the body can be called "fear" or "excitement," so, too, the energy of achievement can be called *creative, sexual* or *spiritual.*

Creativity can solve almost any problem.
The creative act,
the defeat of habit by originality,
overcomes everything.

GEORGE LOIS

315

123

When we direct this energy of achievement toward anything, it becomes *passion*. Most people have their passion hard-wired (and often hot-wired) toward a particular thing. It might be a person, certain foods, a given TV program, sex, money, football, macramé—whatever. The list of things people feel passionate about is almost as long as a list of things.

Success is not the result of spontaneous combustion.
You must set yourself on fire.

REGGIE LEACH

341

*You can have anything you want
if you want it desperately enough.
You must want it with an inner exuberance
that erupts through the skin
and joins the energy that created the world.*

SHEILA GRAHAM

124

What we feel passionate about is our choice. For most of us, however, the choice was made long ago, and we forgot that we chose. We *know* what the choice *is*—the thing we automatically feel passionate about—but we've forgotten having made the choice.

> *Put all your eggs*
> *in one basket and*
> *WATCH THAT BASKET!*
>
> MARK TWAIN

341

If you have built castles in the air,
your work need not be lost;
that is where they should be.
Now put the foundations under them.

HENRY DAVID THOREAU

The hand is the cutting edge of the mind.

JACOB BRONOWSKI

125

You can, however, redirect the passion from something you currently feel passionate about to your Dream. All it takes is (A) remembering to do it, and (B) a *specific* image of your Dream to feel passionate about.

*One person with belief
is equal to a force of
ninety-nine who have only interests.*

JOHN STUART MILL

343

126

The biggest lie we tell ourselves in the area of action is, "I'll do it later."

Delay is the deadliest form of denial.
C. NORTHCOTE PARKINSON

367

127

The interesting thing about "later" is that it can never be proven false. One can never reproach us. If confronted, we can always say, "I said I'd do it later. It's not later yet."

If you trap the moment before it's ripe,
The tears of repentance you'll certainly wipe;
But if once you let the ripe moment go
You can never wipe off the tears of woe.

WILLIAM BLAKE

367

128

If you can do something now, do it now. If it can't be done now, decide (A) it's not going to get done, or (B) *when* it will get done.

Laziness is nothing more than the habit of resting before you get tired.

JULES RENARD

367

129

A primary reason people don't do new things is because they want to be able to do them perfectly—first time. It's completely irrational, impractical, not workable—and yet, it's how most people run their lives. It's called The Perfection Syndrome.

Have no fear of perfection—you'll never reach it.

SALVADOR DALI

371

130

Whoever said we had to do it perfect? Just DO IT!

When in doubt, make a fool of yourself.
There is a microscopically thin line
between being brilliantly creative and
acting like the most gigantic idiot on earth.
So what the hell, leap.

CYNTHIA HEIMEL

371

131

Enough! It's time to grow up. If we want to play adult games—living our Dream—we must play by adult rules. One of the primary adult rules: We are individually responsible for our own lives.

Creativity represents a miraculous coming together
of the uninhibited energy of the child
with its apparent opposite and enemy,
the sense of order imposed on
the disciplined adult intelligence.

NORMAN PODHORETZ

387

132

Responsibility simply means, "The ability to respond." In any of life's challenges, opportunities or disasters, we can *respond* in whatever way we choose. It's not a matter of right/wrong, good/bad. It's a matter of *practical analysis* of the situation.

> *There's nothing to winning, really.*
> *That is, if you happen to be blessed with*
> *a keen eye, an agile mind,*
> *and no scruples whatsoever.*
>
> ALFRED HITCHCOCK

387

133

In addition to what we can do *physically* about a situation, we also have the ability to choose what our *inner* response to that situation is.

> *The greatest discovery of my generation*
> *is that a human being can alter his life by*
> *altering his attitudes of mind.*
>
> WILLIAM JAMES
> (1842–1910)

387

134

This is a big one. It sounds like a radical new idea, but it's not. It's centuries old. The idea is this: what happens in the outer environment has *nothing to do* with how we *respond* to what happens in the outer environment.

If you are distressed by anything external,
the pain is not due to the thing itself,
but to your estimate of it;
and this you have the power to revoke at any moment.

MARCUS AURELIUS

389

135

It is OK to feel good when things go bad. Being content, satisfied and joyful no matter *what* happens is a radical concept—but it's also a basic rule of adult life.

An Englishman thinks he is moral
when he is only uncomfortable.

GEORGE BERNARD SHAW

When I was born
I was so surprised
I didn't talk
for a year and a half.

GRACIE ALLEN

389

136

We don't plan to fail, we just fail to plan. So, plan. And, be prepared not just to change *horses* in midstream, but to change to a *boat* in midstream. Keep your goal, your Dream. Stay firm and fixed on that. Be prepared, however, for whatever methods come along to get you there. *Especially* methods not on your plan. Plan on it.

Next week there can't be any crisis.
My schedule is already full.

HENRY A. KISSINGER

393

137

Someone once said, "A blank sheet of paper is God's way of letting you know what it feels like to be God." So is a blank calendar. A calendar for the next year represents your *time*, one of the most precious commodities you have. Use it well. Choosing what you want to do, and when to do it, is an act of creation. You are creating your Dream.

> *I've been on a calendar,*
> *but I've never been on time.*
>
> MARILYN MONROE

397

A lot of successful people are risk-takers.
Unless you're willing to do that,
to have a go,
to fail miserably,
and have another go,
success won't happen.

PHILIP ADAMS

138

As often as we are counseled to "take risks" by the success-ful people of the world, that's about as often as that counsel is ignored. For the vast, vast majority of people, taking risks is just too, well, *risky.* If we don't take risks, however, it's doubtful we'll ever get to our Dream.

Once you accept your own death,
all of a sudden
you're free to live.
You no longer care about your reputation.
You no longer care except so far as
your life can be used tactically—
to promote a cause you believe in.

SAUL ALINSKY

401

139

The irony is that the person *not* taking risks feels the same amount of fear as the person who *regularly* takes risks. The non-risk-taker simply feels the *same* amount of fear over more *trivial* things.

*Every man has the right
to risk his own life
in order to save it.*

JEAN-JACQUES ROUSSEAU

401

140

People not taking calculated risks, designed to pursue their Dream, sometimes take foolish risks. They drive too fast, drink too much, abuse drugs, or engage in some other reckless behavior.

Take calculated risks.
That is quite different from being rash.

GEORGE PATTON

A cardinal rule of politics—
never get caught in bed with a live man or a dead woman.

J. R. EWING
"DALLAS"

403

141

When we commit to a goal, the methods to achieve that goal will appear. When the methods do appear, they may not be (and seldom are) dressed in familiar garb. Many people are in the habit of saying "no" to all new experiences. Don't say no till you know what you're saying no to.

The greatest obstacle to discovery is not ignorance—
it is the illusion of knowledge.

DANIEL J. BOORSTIN

405

142

Your goal-fulfillment system is working all the time—pulling experiences, lessons, information and people to you to help you fulfill your Dream.

Let your hook always be cast.
In the pool where you least expect it, will be a fish.

OVID

409

143

Mistakes show us what we need to learn. They indicate what we must study in order to have success. When we make a mistake, it's a golden arrow saying, "Study this if you want success."

From error to error, one discovers the entire truth.
SIGMUND FREUD

144

Many people read about the value of mistakes, say, "That makes sense," and then continue living their lives in the same avoid-mistakes-at-all-costs manner as before. They continue to play it safe, don't learn what they need to know, and then wonder why they're not closer to their Dream.

*Try everything once
except incest and folk dancing.*

SIR THOMAS BEECHAM

411

Inside the ears of crazy people:
Go to the zoo and enlist.
Shave your neighbor's dog.
Yo! Dump your spaghetti on that guy's head.

GARY LARSON

I owe my success to
having listened respectfully
to the very best advice,
and then going away
and doing the exact opposite.

G. K. CHESTERTON

145

The process of learning can be given in four steps:

1. Act.

2. Look for the mistakes (criticize, evaluate).

3. Learn how to do it better next time.

4. Go to 1.

> *You will make all kinds of mistakes;*
> *but as long as you are generous and true,*
> *and also fierce,*
> *you cannot hurt the world*
> *or even seriously distress her.*

SIR WINSTON CHURCHILL

413

146

Distractions do not bring satisfaction. Let go of them. What are distractions? Anything not on the way to our goal that consumes our time, thoughts or emotional energy is a distraction.

> *The sun will set without thy assistance.*
> THE TALMUD

415

147

The distractions do *anything they want* to tempt you off your path: offer sex, food, fame, power, success in an area not part of your Dream, recognition, easy money—*anything*. What they *cannot* do is get *on* your path and *stop you*. Leaving the path is always *your choice*. Choose to pursue your Dream. Follow your path.

Never give in.
Never. Never. Never. Never.

SIR WINSTON CHURCHILL

148

It is your job to fulfill your Dream.

> *My philosophy is that
> not only are you responsible
> for your life,
> but doing the best
> at this moment
> puts you in the best place
> for the next moment.*

OPRAH WINFREY

417

149

Pursuing your Dream requires work—mental, emotional and physical. Work is what we don't want to do, but we do anyway to get something else. To reach your Dream, you'll be called upon to do a lot of things you don't want to do.

Opportunity is missed by most people
because it is dressed in overalls
and looks like work.

THOMAS EDISON

421

150

How do we know when it was enough? Simple. When we have what we want, it was enough. Until then, it wasn't. Do the work until it's enough—until you have your Dream.

Do something every day that you don't want to do.
This is the golden rule for acquiring
the habit of doing your duty without pain.

MARK TWAIN

423

151

Consider the pursuit of your dream a major athletic event. Train for it. What we do we become stronger in. That's true mentally, emotionally, and physically.

Physically: Keep fit.

Emotions: Keep them flexible.

Mind: Keep it open.

Comfort Zone: Keep expanding it.

> *Only Irish coffee provides in a single glass*
> *all four essential food groups:*
> *alcohol, caffeine, sugar, and fat.*
>
> ALEX LEVINE

427

152

Nothing is impossible. The more *improbable* something is, however, the more work it takes to achieve.

*The one unchangeable certainty is that
nothing is unchangeable or certain.*

JOHN F. KENNEDY

431

153

Keep track of your successes—the achievement of the interim goals on the way to the Big One. Record them in some way. As this list grows, it becomes a testament to your power, your creativity, your achievement. (Besides, in the years to come, your many biographers will appreciate whatever help you can give them.)

Writing is easy.
All you do is stare at a blank sheet of paper
until drops of blood form on your forehead.

GENE FOWLER

433

154

People, books, tapes, videos, magazines, etc. are all short-cuts to success.

Learn from the accumulated wisdom of the ages. That's what it's been accumulating for.

*The journey of ten thousand miles
begins with a single phone call.*

CONFUCIUS BELL

435

155

In following *your* Dream, you will probably notice that you have more rules than ever before. What's going on? Isn't your Dream supposed to bring *freedom?* Yes, and freedom is found in discipline.

> *In the last analysis,*
> *our only freedom*
> *is the freedom*
> *to discipline ourselves.*
>
> BERNARD BARUCH

437

156

Discipline comes from the word *disciple*—being a devoted student. Think of discipline as a container. Once a container is constructed—and maintained—it can envelop your Dream.

*Take what you can use
and let the rest go by.*

KEN KESEY

437

157

Begin to formulate your own set of "rules" on how *you* best achieve dreams. To fulfill our Dream, we need only examine our life, and do two things:

1. More of what works.

2. Less of what doesn't.

I've got to keep breathing.
It'll be my worst business mistake if I don't.

SIR NATHAN MEYER ROTHSCHILD

439

158

It's important to nurture yourself while you're nurturing your Dream. In the large sense, of course, pursuing your dream *is* nurturing yourself. Along the way to your Dream, however, take time to be good to yourself.

> *I'm at an age where I think*
> *more about food than sex.*
> *Last week I put a mirror*
> *over my dining room table.*

RODNEY DANGERFIELD

441

159

Succumbing to the comfort zone's demands is *not* "taking care of yourself." Nurturing yourself means taking care of yourself *while you do what needs to be done*. This might mean working twenty hours on a project you *could* complete in fifteen. It does *not* mean not doing the project.

*Advice to expectant mothers: you must remember that
when you are pregnant, you are eating for two.
But you must remember that the other one of you
is about the size of a golf ball, so let's not go overboard with it.
I mean, a lot of pregnant women eat as though
the other person they're eating for is Orson Welles.*

DAVE BARRY

441

160

Rehabilitate your attitude toward words such as "work," "vacation" and "time off." The idea that we need "time off" comes from working for another to fulfill another's dreams. Now your life is directed toward fulfilling *your* Dream. Why would you want to take "time off" from that?

INTERVIEWER:
Your Holiness, how many people work in the Vatican?

POPE JOHN XXIII:
About half.

441

161

Learn to seek *satisfaction* in a job well done, rather than seek diversion in activities designed to distract you from the "harsh reality of work."

I don't have anything against work.
I just figure, why deprive somebody who really loves it?

DOBIE GILLIS

The more I want to get something done,
the less I call it work.

RICHARD BACH

441

162

True nurturing is learning to enjoy the path, the process, the journey toward your Dream.

If A is success in life,
then A equals X plus Y plus Z.
Work is X,
Y is play,
and Z is keeping your mouth shut.

ALBERT EINSTEIN

Keep walking and keep smiling.

TINY TIM

441

163

Nothing succeeds like **persistence.** The common denominator of *all* successful people is their persistence.

Nothing in the world can take the place of persistence.
Talent will not;
nothing is more common than unsuccessful men with talent.
Genius will not;
unrewarded genius is almost a proverb.
Education alone will not;
the world is full of educated derelicts.
Persistence and determination alone are omnipotent.

CALVIN COOLIDGE

443

164

Persistence is a simple process:

1. What's the next step?
2. What's in the way of taking that step?
3. Remove, disregard, or ignore the obstacle.
4. Take the step.
5. Go to 1.

Fall seven times, stand up eight.
JAPANESE PROVERB

445

165

Rather than "comfort and joy," try *enthusiasm* and joy. Enthusiasm and joy are Siamese twins—it's hard to find one without the other. Enthusiasm comes from the Latin *en theos*—one with the energy of the Divine. The way to create joy is to do things joyfully.

The real secret of success is enthusiasm.
WALTER CHRYSLER

447

166

1. Find your horse.

2. Discover the direction the horse is going.

3. Ride the horse in that direction.

Happy trails!

Saddle your dreams afore you ride 'em.

MARY WEBB
(1881–1927)

449

167

When we know how easy it is to fulfill a Dream (easy compared with how *impossible* most people believe it to be), we know we *can* do it—we *can* take the Dream for our own. Once we are free to take it, we are free to leave it.

*A man is rich in proportion to the number of things
which he can afford to let alone.*

HENRY DAVID THOREAU

457

168

After fulfilling a Dream or two (or twenty), we will be called upon to pass on some of what we have learned to others. This can be in many forms. Just as, "When the student is ready, the teacher appears," so, too, "When the teacher is ready, the student appears."

I've always thought that the
stereotype of the dirty old man
is really the creation of a dirty young man
who wants the field to himself.

HUGH DOWNS

459

169

After obtaining several material Dreams, you may wonder, "Where are these Dreams coming from?" Important question. Seeking the answer to that question may begin an important inner quest. What we learn from fulfilling Dreams in the outer world can be used for pursuing Dreams within ourselves.

> *To know oneself*
> *one should assert oneself.*
>
> ALBERT CAMUS

461

170

When people give to themselves—when they fulfill their own Dreams—they are filled to overflowing. There are two interesting things about the overflow: (1) it is abundant, and (2) it can't be stored. What can one do with the overflow?

> *We are here on earth to do good to others.*
> *What the others are here for, I don't know.*

W. H. AUDEN

463

171

And there we have one of the great open secrets of life: giving to others gives us more than we give away. When people discover this, there's no stopping them.

The common idea that success spoils people
by making them vain, egotistic,
and self-complacent is erroneous.
On the contrary, it makes them,
for the most part,
humble, tolerant and kind.
Failure makes people bitter and cruel.

SOMERSET MAUGHAM

463

172

We will close with this from Guillaume Apollinaire—

"Come to the edge," he said.
They said, "We are afraid."
"Come to the edge," he said.
They came.
He pushed them
And they flew.

471

*For more information on
our books and unabridged audio tapes,
please write to*

*Prelude Press
8159 Santa Monica Boulevard
Los Angeles, California 90046*

or call

1-800-LIFE-101

Thank you!

Index

*Here I am
at the end of the road,
at the top of the heap.*

POPE JOHN XXIII